Airplanes

BY CYNTHIA AMOROSO

The Child's World

Published by The Child's World®
1980 Lookout Drive • Mankato, MN 56003-1705
800-599-READ • www.childsworld.com

Acknowledgments
The Child's World®: Mary Berendes, Publishing Director
The Design Lab: Design
Jody Jensen Shaffer: Editing
Pamela J. Mitsakos: Photo Research

Photos
ansonsaw/iStock.com: cover, 1;
carlosphotoscarlosphotos/iStock.com: 12;
FrankvandenBergh/iStock.com: 16; gchutka/iStock.com:
15; MC_PP/Shutterstock.com: 20; Mikhail Starodubov/
Shutterstock.com; 7; Mikulas Jaros/iStock.com: 11;
MoiseevVladislav/iStock.com: 4; Portokalis/Shutterstock.
com: 19; Vincent St. Thomas/Shutterstock.com: 8

ISBN 9781623239619
LCCN 2013947246

Printed in the United States of America
Mankato, MN
November, 2013
PA02190

Contents

Jets like this one carry lots of people.

What are airplanes?

Airplanes are **vehicles** that fly. Some carry only one or two people. Others carry hundreds of people. Airplanes can go faster than cars.

What are the parts of an airplane?

Airplanes have wings. They have a tail. They have a body, called the **fuselage**. People or goods ride in the fuselage. Underneath the fuselage is the **landing gear**.

fuselage

landing gear

This airplane has two engines on each wing.

Airplanes are powered by **engines**. Most large airplanes have jet engines. So do some small airplanes. Other airplanes have engines with **propellers** instead. Both kinds of engines push the airplane forward.

How do airplanes fly?

As the plane moves forward, air races past the wings. The wings are a special shape. The shape makes the moving air push them upward. The plane lifts off the ground. The air holds the plane up.

This airplane has a propeller on the front.

Pilots must know how to use all of an airplane's controls.

Who flies airplanes?

In the front of the airplane is the **cockpit**. That is where the **pilot** sits. The pilot flies the plane. Sometimes other people help fly the plane, too.

How are airplanes used?

Airplanes often carry **passengers**. People use airplanes to fly all over the world. They use them to fly on vacations. They use them to travel for work. Flying is often the quickest way to travel.

Some passengers can sit by a window and look outside.

Cargo is often packed in big bundles.

16

Many airplanes carry **cargo** instead of people. Businesses use airplanes to move packages quickly. The postal service uses airplanes to carry mail. Airplanes carry everything from toys to big machines.

Airplanes are used for other things, too. Many countries have planes in their armies and navies. Some airplanes help firefighters put out forest fires. Others dust farm fields to kill weeds or pests. Some planes are used to put on shows for people.

This airplane
is dropping water
on a forest fire.

This airplane is taking off for a faraway city.

Are airplanes important?

Airplanes are used every day, all over the world. They are used for business. They are used for fun. They carry goods from one place to another. They move things and people quickly. They are very important!

GLOSSARY

cargo (KAR-go) Cargo is gear or goods carried by a vehicle.

cockpit (KOK-pit) The cockpit is the area of a plane or boat where the pilot sits.

engines (EN-junz) Engines are machines that make things move.

fuselage (FYOO-seh-lazh) The body of an airplane is called its fuselage.

landing gear (LAND-ing GEER) Landing gear is machinery and wheels on which an airplane lands.

passengers (PASS-un-jurz) People who ride in something are called passengers.

pilot (PY-lut) A pilot is a person who flies an airplane or steers a ship.

propellers (pru-PEL-lurz) Propellers are nearly flat blades that spin quickly to move a vehicle.

vehicles (VEE-uh-kulz) Vehicles are things for carrying people or goods.

BOOKS

Bingham, Caroline. *DK Big Book of Airplanes.* New York: Dorling Kindersley, 2001.

Evans, Frank, and George Guzzi (illustrator). *All Aboard Airplanes.* New York: Grosset & Dunlap, 1994.

Shields, Amy. *National Geographic Readers: Planes.* Washington, DC: National Geographic, 2010.

WEB SITES

Visit our Web site for lots of links about airplanes:
childsworld.com/links

Note to parents, teachers, and librarians: We routinely check our Web links to make sure they're safe, active sites—so encourage your readers to check them out!

INDEX

ABOUT THE AUTHOR

Even as a child, Cynthia Amoroso knew she wanted to be a writer. She is always working to involve kids in reading and writing, and she loves spending time in the children's section of the library or bookstore. Cynthia enjoys gardening, traveling, and having fun with friends and family.